Released for Purpose

Breaking Chains, Unlocking Destiny

By

Kirk D. Campbell

Acknowledgments

Every book is a journey, and no journey is ever walked alone.

When I began writing *Released for Purpose: Breaking Chains, Unlocking Destiny*, I believed I was simply putting my message into words. What I discovered instead was that writing this book became part of my own healing, growth, and transformation. This work was not created in isolation. It was shaped through prayer, reflection, and the stories of people who trusted me with their truth. What you hold in your hands is not the product of one person's vision, but the fruit of many hearts aligned toward freedom and faith.

To God

First and foremost, I give all honor and glory to my Lord and Savior, Jesus Christ. Without His grace, guidance, and sustaining power, this book would not exist. Every word reflects His purpose working through me. To Him be all the praise.

To My Family

To my wonderful wife, **Alison**, and our two sons, **Luke** and **Liam**, thank you for your love, patience, and unwavering support. You are my greatest earthly blessings and constant reminders of God's faithfulness. Your encouragement has steadied me through long nights of writing and seasons of deep reflection.

To my mother, **Lorna Stewart**, thank you for your strength and sacrifices. You taught me what it means to persevere and to trust that purpose can grow even in hard places.

To my sister, **Sharon Campbell**, and my brother, **Anthony Robinson**, thank you for being part of the foundation of my life. Family remains one of God's greatest gifts, and I am grateful for the one He placed me in.

To My First Church Family

To my **Faith Miracle Temple** family, thank you for being the soil where my faith took root. It was there that I gave my life to Christ, was baptized, and married my wife. Those early years of worship, service, and community formed the foundation of my spiritual journey. You taught me what it means to belong, to grow, and to serve with humility and joy.

To My Church Family

To my **Kennedy Road Tabernacle** family, thank you for being the community where my faith continues to deepen and my calling matures. Your prayers, encouragement, and spiritual covering have sustained me. You have created a space where faith and authenticity thrive, and I am grateful to walk this journey among you.

To My Brothers

To the **Caledon Iron Sharpens Iron** Men's Bible Study Group, thank you for your brotherhood, honesty, and accountability. You have sharpened my faith, challenged my thinking, and strengthened my character. Iron truly does sharpen iron, and you have sharpened me more than you know.

To My Spiritual Leaders

To all my pastors, both past and present, thank you for teaching me that leadership is not performance but presence, not perfection but faithfulness. Your wisdom and example have helped shape my calling and my character.

To My Colleagues and Mentors

To my colleagues and mentors, thank you for your insight, encouragement, and friendship. You have taught me that excellence and faith can coexist, and that integrity in the workplace is a form of worship.

To My Extended Family and Friends

To my extended family and friends, thank you for your love, laughter, and the countless ways you have influenced my life. Your encouragement and kindness have carried me farther than words can express. You have celebrated my victories, stood with me in challenges, and reminded me that I am never alone.

From the depths of my heart, thank you all. Your prayers, love, and support have been instruments in the hands of God, shaping both the message and the mission behind this book. Each of you has played a part in helping me live the very principles found within these pages.

May God bless you richly for the ways you have poured into my life.

With gratitude and honor,

Kirk D. Campbell

Foreword

It is an honor to write this foreword for my long-time friend, Kirk D. Campbell. Kirk and his wife, Alison, along with their family, were active members of the church I pastored in Toronto, Canada. It was a joy to watch them grow in faith, in family, and in wisdom. When I heard that Kirk was writing a book, I was eager to read what God had placed in his heart.

There are books you read, and then there are books that read you. Released for Purpose: Breaking Chains, Unlocking Destiny belongs in that latter category. As I read it, it felt as though I was holding up a mirror to my heart. We live in a world that often pressures people to change through shame, but Kirk reminds us that God has already placed divine potential within us. That potential has been quietly fighting to breathe beneath the weight of fear, pain, and delay.

This book reflects what God has done in Kirk's own life. He has discovered what remains eternally true: Jesus is still the Chain Breaker. What the enemy meant for harm, God transforms into purpose. Many people believe that God has a plan for their life (Jeremiah 29:11), yet they feel stuck in memories they cannot forgive, unaware of the gifts that lie dormant within them, and afraid to take the next step. Each chapter of this book shines light on the path to freedom:

- Unmasking fear so its lies lose power

- Choosing forgiveness to heal the heart

- Discovering hidden treasure in what God has already placed within

- Courageously stepping toward destiny, not someday, but today

This is not just another motivational book. Within these pages are biblically grounded strategies for personal transformation. They replace excuses with truth and help build unshakable faith. It is no accident that you are reading this book. God creates divine moments like this, moments when a single step of obedience unlocks destiny.

Open your heart. There is a future already written in Heaven with your name on it. Chains will break. Gifts will emerge. Destiny will rise.

This is your moment. Welcome to the journey.

Dr. Jamie Stewart (Rev.)

Lead Pastor, Life Church

Kissimmee, FL

Table of Contents

Introduction

Thank you for choosing this book. I hope that these words ignite courage within you… Your release begins here.

This book is more than words on a page, it is an invitation. An invitation to step into the unique life God designed for you. My prayer is both simple and profound: that as you read, chains will break, hope will rise, and the God-given destiny within you will awaken with fresh fire.

I write these pages not merely as an author but as a fellow traveler on the journey of faith. I know what it feels like to wrestle with fear, to carry the weight of setbacks, and to wonder whether purpose still waits on the other side of pain. Yet I also know this: Jesus Christ, my Lord and Savior, is a chain breaker, a restorer, and the One who breathes destiny into dry places. His grace has marked every chapter of my life, and it is His grace that fuels every word you'll encounter here.

I am deeply blessed to share this life with my wonderful wife, Alison Sealy-Campbell, and together we are the proud parents of two incredible sons, Luke and Liam. They remind me daily of God's faithfulness, of the legacy we carry, and of the calling to live a life of impact that extends beyond ourselves.

Professionally, I have spent decades as a certified Project Management Professional (PMP®), leading complex, multi-million-dollar projects in both private corporations and within the Government of Canada. Yet beyond deadlines, boardrooms, and strategy sessions, my truest calling has always been to serve. For over twenty years, I have walked the halls of correctional institutions across Ontario, Canada, ministering to men and women carrying heavy chains of regret and loss. There, in those spaces of brokenness, I have witnessed firsthand the unstoppable power of the gospel, a power that transforms despair into destiny.

God has also opened doors for me to serve through short-term missions in Cuba, New York, and across Canada. Whether across oceans or across the street, the call has always been the same: to proclaim the good news of Jesus Christ and to witness His transforming power at work in ordinary lives.

As you turn these pages, I invite you to see your own story reflected in these principles and testimonies. You may feel as though you are holding only broken pieces, but in God's hands, those pieces can become a testimony of freedom and a roadmap to destiny. No chain is too strong for Him to break. No past is too heavy for Him to redeem. No dream is too distant for Him to fulfill.

Thank you for choosing this book. My hope is that these words ignite courage within you to believe again, passion to rise again, and determination to walk boldly into the future God has already written for you.

Welcome to the journey. Your release begins here.

Chapter One

Recognize - Unmasking Fear's Deception

When Fear Wears a Mask

The screen glared back at me like a silent judge. One press of the delete key, and months of work would vanish. Fear leaned in close and whispered, "End this. You are not a writer. Stop embarrassing yourself."

For a moment, I almost believed it.

Pause with me here. What came to your mind as you read those words? Perhaps a book you never finished. A business idea you buried. A calling you delayed. That tug you feel isn't random; it is destiny knocking, waiting to see if you will open the door.

Research shows most people die with their dreams still locked inside them. I almost became one of them. The graveyard, they say, is the richest place on earth, filled with unwritten books, unstarted businesses, and songs never sung. I was dangerously close to adding my contribution to that silent cemetery of possibilities.

Unmasking Fear

Fear rarely storms in with loud threats. More often, it sneaks in quietly, disguised as logic. It asks questions that sound reasonable: Do you really have what it takes? Who do you think you are? What if you fail and everyone sees it?

These aren't just casual questions. They're surgical strikes aimed at your identity, your calling, your confidence. Fear knows exactly where to cut deepest, and it wields doubt like a scalpel, making precise incisions in places you thought were healed.

But beneath the disguise, fear is always the same thing: a thief. Its only purpose is to rob what God has planted in your heart. Jesus warned us about thieves: "The thief comes only to steal and kill and destroy" (John 10:10). Fear operates with the same agenda, stealing your courage, killing your dreams, destroying your potential before it can take root.

The Bible unmasks fear clearly: "God has not given us a spirit of fear, but of power, love, and a sound mind" (2 Timothy 1:7). Fear is not divine caution; it is counterfeit wisdom designed to keep you bound. When you feel that paralyzing dread, that's not God speaking. God's voice may challenge you, stretch you, even make you uncomfortable, but it always empowers, never paralyzes.

The Science of Fear

The American Psychological Association reports that 75 percent of people fear public speaking, and 68 percent admit they avoid opportunities because they fear failure.

Neuroscientist Dr. Joseph LeDoux notes that most fears are learned responses, not instinctive protections.

In other words, fear is not truth; it is often a habit we inherit, not a command we must obey. Think about that. The very thing holding you back may be a borrowed belief, passed down through generations, or absorbed from past disappointments. You're obeying an order you never agreed to follow.

Fear manipulates through three primary weapons that show up in real scenarios:

The Voice of False Logic appears when you're about to apply for that promotion: "Be realistic. Look at your background compared to the other candidates. Who do you think you are?" It masquerades as wisdom while enforcing limitation, convincing you to withdraw your application before you even try. This voice sounds so reasonable, so mature, so responsible. That's what makes it deadly. It dresses cowardice in the language of prudence.

The Mirror of Comparison strikes when you see a colleague's success on social media. Suddenly, your steady progress feels insignificant. Fear forces you to measure your behind-the-scenes struggles against their highlight reel moments, ensuring you always feel inadequate and questioning your own path. You're comparing your rough draft to someone else's published edition, and fear makes sure you never notice the difference.

The Clock of Urgency whispers when you finally feel ready to start that business at 45: "It's too late. You should have done this in your twenties. All the good ideas are taken." It convinces you that timing has disqualified you, when God's timing is never late, and experience often trumps youth. Colonel Sanders was 62 when he franchised KFC. Vera Wang entered fashion design at 40. Moses was 80 when God called him to lead. Your timeline is not your disqualification; it's your preparation.

The Modern Face of Fear: Job Displacement

Today, fear has found a new weapon in the rapid advancement of technology, particularly Artificial Intelligence.

As a certified Project Management Professional, I've spent decades watching technology transform industries. But nothing prepared me for the avalanche of warnings that began flooding my professional world. AI will replace millions of jobs. Entire industries will be automated overnight. Even project management, my field of expertise, faces potential disruption.

The headlines were relentless: "AI Could Replace 40% of Jobs Within 15 Years." "Artificial Intelligence: The End of

Human Work?" Industry leaders painted apocalyptic pictures at conferences I attended. Some predicted that even strategic roles like mine could be reduced to algorithms.

I'll be honest, it shook me. Late at night, I found myself wondering: Have I built my career on shifting sand? Will the skills I've honed over decades become irrelevant? The whisper was familiar, though dressed in modern language: *You're about to become obsolete.*

But then God reminded me of a truth that cuts through every wave of technological advancement: He is my provider, not my profession. My security has never rested in project management certifications or corporate titles; it rests in the One who "supplies every need according to His riches in glory" (Philippians 4:19).

What fear won't tell you is this: every major technological leap in history created anxiety about job displacement before it created new opportunities. When the Industrial Revolution mechanized manufacturing, people feared mass unemployment. When computers arrived, critics predicted they would eliminate countless jobs. When the internet transformed commerce, many worried entire industries would collapse. Each time, fear's voice was loud and urgent.

And each time, innovation created new types of work that hadn't existed before. The telegraph operators became telephone workers. The bookkeepers became data analysts. The factory workers became machine operators and engineers. History teaches us that human adaptability always outpaces technological disruption.

AI will be no different.

Disruption Creates Opportunity

Yes, AI will change the way we work. But it will also open doors we cannot yet imagine. Routine tasks are already being automated. That simply clears more space for what only humans can bring: creativity, empathy, leadership, and spiritual discernment.

Machines can calculate, but they cannot call. They can generate text, but they cannot carry your testimony. They can simulate empathy, but they cannot reveal the love of Christ working through you. They can process information, but they cannot impart wisdom born from walking through fire and emerging refined.

Oprah Winfrey didn't transform media because of superior technology. She did it because she connected with people at the level of the soul. The same will be true in the age of AI. Technology shapes the tools. Purpose shapes the impact.

Leadership expert John Maxwell says it plainly: "Courage is not the absence of fear; it's moving forward in spite of it."

Fear says AI will erase your relevance. Faith says God can use it as a platform to amplify your purpose if you walk with courage. The same God who has provided through every technological shift will provide through this one, too. He didn't bring you this far to abandon you at the threshold of innovation.

The Day I Refused to Hide

Eventually, I realized something sobering: fear never steps aside voluntarily. It waits for you to surrender.

That morning, my hands trembled on the keyboard, but I wrote anyway. My pulse thundered as new opportunities came, but I said yes anyway. Each act of obedience was like striking a hammer against fear's mask, breaking it piece by piece.

Courage is not waiting for fear to vanish. Courage is choosing to move forward while fear screams from the sidelines. David didn't wait until Goliath looked smaller. He ran toward him while his knees still shook. Peter didn't wait until the water felt solid. He stepped out while the waves still threatened to swallow him.

The Bible promises: "Do not fear, for I am with you; do not be dismayed, for I am your God. I will strengthen you and help you" (Isaiah 41:10). Fear thrives in isolation, but it dies when we remember that God Himself goes with us into every space.

Stepping Out Anyway

Your dream may terrify you. That does not disqualify you. In fact, it may prove you are closer to destiny than you realize. Fear screams loudest when purpose is near.

Oprah was told she was unfit for television. She stepped forward anyway.

And me? For ten years, fear told me this book should never be written. The idea first came as a seed a decade ago, burning quietly inside me. Every time I thought of starting, fear whispered, "You are not ready." You are not qualified. No one will read it. So, I delayed. I disguised procrastination as wisdom.

But here's the miracle, you are holding the very book fear tried to bury. What fear postponed for ten years, God has now brought to life. The pages in your hands are living proof that fear never gets the final word. Every sentence you read is a victory over the voice that said it couldn't be done.

And if God could bring my delayed seed to fruition, what could He do with yours? What dream has been waiting in the soil of your soul, needing only the courage to break through?

Steps to Break Fear's Hold

Step One: Name your fear. Write it down. Be specific. Expose it to the light. Fear loses power when dragged from the shadow into the truth.

Step Two: Replace the lie with truth. When fear says technology will erase your purpose, declare: "I am God's workmanship, created in Christ Jesus for good works, which God prepared in advance for me to, do" (Ephesians 2:10). Speak it aloud. Let your ears hear what your heart knows.

The Seeds That Refuse to Die

There's something you need to understand about God-given dreams: they possess an unusual resilience. You can bury them under years of excuses, cover them with layers of fear, even try to forget they ever existed. But like seeds beneath winter snow, they remain alive, waiting for the right season to break through.

I learned this truth the hard way. During those ten years of delay, I convinced myself the dream had died. I told myself that missed opportunities were closed doors, that hesitation was discernment, that "someday" was a legitimate timeline. But deep in quiet moments, usually at 3 AM when pretense falls away, I felt it: that persistent stirring that wouldn't let me rest.

That's how you know the difference between a passing interest and a divine assignment. Passing interests fade when ignored. Divine assignments intensify.

What Fear Costs Us

Let me be brutally honest about what those ten years of hesitation cost me. It wasn't just a delayed book. It was ten years of people I could have helped but didn't. Ten years of conversations that could have sparked transformation. Ten years of testimony locked in silence while others struggled with the same battles I had already fought. Fear doesn't just rob you. It robs everyone connected to your purpose.

When Moses stood before the burning bush, he offered God a list of reasons why he was unqualified. God's response wasn't to remove Moses' limitations; it was to remind him: "I will be with you" (Exodus 3:12). The issue was never Moses' ability. It was his willingness to move despite feeling inadequate.

The same applies to you. Your dream doesn't require perfection. It requires participation.

Breaking the Paralysis

Here's what finally broke my decade-long paralysis: I stopped asking, "What if I fail?" and started asking, "What if I succeed, and my delay meant someone suffered longer than necessary?"

That question changed everything.

Suddenly, my fear of failure seemed selfish compared to someone else's need for a breakthrough. My comfort zone became uncomfortable when I realized it was a cage not just for me, but for everyone waiting on the other side of my obedience.

Author Steven Pressfield calls this "Resistance," that invisible force that shows up most powerfully when we're about to do something that matters. He writes, "The more important a call or action is to our soul's evolution, the more Resistance we will feel toward pursuing it."

Fear has held its position long enough. It's time to dismantle it systematically, step by step, letter by letter. Let's deploy the F.E.A.R. principle today.

F - Face It Honestly

The first step is the hardest: Stop disguising it. Stop calling it by softer names like "caution" or "wisdom" or "bad timing." Face your fear honestly and name it specifically. David faced Goliath by walking straight toward him, not by pretending the giant wasn't there. Your giant loses its advantage the moment you stop avoiding eye contact.

E - Examine Its Source

Once you've faced your fear, ask the crucial question: Where did this come from? Fear rarely originates from divine wisdom. More often, it stems from past wounds, inherited beliefs, or cultural conditioning.

Did someone tell you that you weren't smart enough, creative enough, or qualified enough? Did you experience failure before and now assume every attempt will end the same way? Did you absorb limiting beliefs from parents, teachers, or society that shaped how you see yourself?

A - Activate Faith

Fear and faith cannot occupy the same space. When faith increases, fear must decrease. But faith isn't passive wishful thinking; it's active trust that moves your feet even when your heart is pounding.

Activate faith by declaring God's promises over your situation. Not as empty mantras, but as spiritual weapons. "I can do all things through Christ who strengthens me" (Philippians 4:13). "The Lord is my helper; I will not fear" (Hebrews 13:6). "He who began a good work in me will complete it" (Philippians 1:6).

R - Repeat Until Breakthrough

Here's the part nobody wants to hear: you will have to do this more than once. Fear doesn't surrender after a single defeat. It regroups, changes tactics, and comes back wearing a different mask.

That's why the final step is repeated. Face it honestly. Examine its source. Activate faith. Again. And again. And again. Each time you cycle through this framework, fear's grip weakens. Each time you choose courage over comfort, you build spiritual muscle that makes the next battle easier.

Think of it like physical therapy. One session doesn't heal the injury. But consistent, repeated effort rebuilds strength. The F.E.A.R. principle works the same way. Repetition creates transformation.

Your Move

So here we are, at the end of this first chapter, and I have a question for you: What has fear been whispering to you? What dream have you been postponing? What calling have you been negotiating with?

Because here's what I know now that I didn't know ten years ago: the perfect moment never arrives. Courage isn't born from certainty; it's forged in the decision to move forward without it.

You don't need to have it all figured out. You don't need to see the entire staircase. You just need to take the first step. Faith says that's enough. God specializes in meeting us in motion, not in meditation.

This chapter is called "Recognize" because the first victory over fear is simply seeing it for what it is: a liar, a thief, and an imposter that has no legal right to your destiny.

But before you turn the page, do one thing: identify the one dream, the one step, the one conversation you've been avoiding. Write it down. Speak it out loud because recognition without action is just well-informed procrastination.

Reflection Questions

1. What dream have you delayed because fear convinced you it was impossible, or that technology might outpace you?

2. How could you use tools like AI not as threats, but as multipliers of your gifts and talents to fulfill the purpose for which you were created?

Chapter Two

Embrace – The Liberation of Forgiveness

Embrace – The Liberation of Forgiveness

In Chapter One, we uncovered the masks that fear wears and how it can silently control our choices. Recognizing fear was the first step toward freedom. Yet fear rarely walks alone. Once it takes root, it often invites its closest companion: unforgiveness.

If fear keeps us from stepping forward into God's promises, unforgiveness chains us to the pain of our past. It's a cruel partnership, fear whispers that you're not ready for your future, while unforgiveness insists you're still defined by your past. Together, they create a prison with no visible bars, yet you feel trapped all the same.

That is why the next step on our journey is to embrace the liberation of forgiveness.

A Storm of Betrayal

The same hands that praised God on Sunday threw my life into the storm on Tuesday.

Rain hammered my belongings scattered across the front yard of the apartment complex parking lot. My mattress, dresser, clothes, and textbooks were all soaking in puddles like discarded memories. I fumbled with my key, but it no longer fit the lock that had protected my home just hours earlier.

"You're evicted!" came the voice from behind a curtained window.

The betrayal cut deeper than the cold rain. This was not just any landlord. This was Sister Johnson, a deacon at my church, someone who lifted her hands in worship every Sunday. I had seen her pray for others, serve communion, lead Bible study. We shared the same pews, sang the same hymns, bowed before the same altar. How could someone who served communion also serve me an eviction notice without warning? Without conversation? Without mercy?

That night, a friend offered me a place to stay. I sat quietly in the corner of their living room, wrapped in borrowed warmth and kindness. Yet even in that safe space, something inside me shifted. Hurt began to harden into anger, and anger started to calcify into unforgiveness.

I replayed the scene over and over, the rain, the shock, the humiliation of my life displayed for neighbors to see. Each replay added another layer of bitterness. What I did not realize was that I was constructing my own invisible prison, brick by brick, with every bitter thought and rehearsed offense.

The Five Walls of Unforgiveness

In those moments of hurt, I began building what I now call the Five Walls of Unforgiveness. They feel protective at first, like shelter from further harm. But they quickly become the bars of a prison where you are both the guard and the inmate.

1. The Wall of Replay: You rehearse the offense endlessly, keeping the wound fresh. Your mind becomes a courtroom where you are prosecutor, judge, and jury, presenting evidence, delivering verdicts, and replaying testimonies until the pain feels as raw as the day it happened. This wall tricks you into believing that constant rehearsal will somehow change the outcome. It won't. It only deepens the groove of pain in your soul.

2. The Wall of Resentment: Bitterness spreads like an infection, coloring your view of others and yourself. What begins as justified anger against one person metastasizes into suspicion toward everyone. You start seeing betrayal in innocent gestures, reading malice into neutral words. Resentment repaints your entire world in shades of cynicism and distrust.

3. The Wall of Retaliation: Energy is consumed by plotting revenge instead of building your future. You spend hours imagining the perfect comeback, the ultimate exposure of your offender's hypocrisy, the moment they'll finally understand what they did. Meanwhile, your dreams collect dust, your calling waits unattended, and your purpose languishes. Revenge planning is future stealing.

4. The Wall of Rejection: You close your heart to prevent future hurt, but also block future love. This wall whispers a seductive lie: if you never trust again, you can never be hurt again. But in protecting yourself from potential pain, you also exile yourself from potential joy, meaningful relationships, and the very community God designed you to thrive within.

5. The Wall of Rebellion: You resist God's call to forgive, creating distance between yourself and Him. This is perhaps the most dangerous wall because it positions unforgiveness as a form of justice, even righteousness. "God, you can't ask me to forgive this," becomes our stance. But in refusing to forgive, we step outside the flow of grace that sustains us.

Ephesians 4:32 reminds us: "Be kind and compassionate to one another, forgiving each other, just as in Christ God forgave you." Forgiveness is not a suggestion. It is a command that mirrors the mercy God extends to us. Notice the verse doesn't say "forgive each other if they deserve it" or "forgive each other after they apologize." It says forgive just as Christ forgave you, unconditionally, sacrificially, completely.

Which of these walls have you built? Naming them is the first step to tearing them down. And here's the liberating truth: you don't have to demolish all five at once. Start with recognizing just one. Admission is the beginning of freedom.

The Cost of Unforgiveness

Science confirms what scripture already taught. Bitterness poisons the soul, and the body.

Dr. Everett Worthington, a leading researcher on forgiveness, found that unforgiveness floods the body with stress hormones, weakens the immune system, and accelerates the aging process. When we nurse grudges, our bodies pay the price through elevated blood pressure, increased risk of heart disease, and compromised mental health.

When we hold grudges, our brains stay locked in threat-detection mode. Cortisol rises, anxiety grows, and our bodies age more quickly. We become hypervigilant, seeing danger everywhere, unable to rest even in safe spaces. Our nervous system remains in perpetual emergency, exhausting our reserves and shortening our lives.

But forgiveness can reverse the damage. A 2025 study by Emiliana Simon-Thomas and the Greater Good Science

Center found that practicing forgiveness activates brain regions associated with resilience, empathy, and healing. Forgiveness rewires our neural circuits, lowers stress, and expands compassion. It literally changes our brain chemistry, shifting us from survival mode to thriving mode.

Joyce Meyer often says, "Unforgiveness is like drinking poison and hoping your enemy will die." Holding onto bitterness does not punish the person who wronged us, it only poisons our own hearts. Meanwhile, the person who hurt you may be sleeping peacefully, living their life, completely unaffected by your internal turmoil. Choosing forgiveness releases us from the toxic grip of resentment and allows us to live free.

When Forgiveness Feels Impossible

Forgiveness does not erase pain, but it transforms it. It doesn't rewrite history, but it does change your relationship with that history.

Consider the story of Chris Williams.

On February 9, 2007, a drunk driver killed his pregnant wife and two of his children. In a single moment, his family was shattered. As paramedics worked on the survivors, Chris faced a decision that would define the rest of his life. He could cling to anger, or he could choose forgiveness. That night in the hospital, surrounded by unimaginable loss, he whispered words that stunned everyone: "I forgive the young man who caused this accident."

His loss remained real. The empty chairs at his table didn't suddenly fill. The grief didn't vanish. But forgiveness transformed the story. Chris went on to write, speak, and help others navigate tragedy. His wound became his witness. His pain became a pathway for healing others.

Forgiveness did not minimize his suffering. It multiplied his impact. What could have been a story of bitterness destroying what remained of his life became a testimony of grace restoring purpose from ashes.

When God Asked the Impossible

Years later, as Alison and I planned our wedding, I felt God whisper: *Invite Sister Johnson.*

I recoiled. After what she did? Absolutely not. The nerve of even asking! I had every right to exclude her, every justification to keep that door firmly closed. But the whisper persisted, gentle but insistent, like a knock that wouldn't stop.

When I told Alison, she surprised me. "If God is asking," she said, "maybe we should listen."

So we sent the invitation, my hand trembling as I addressed the envelope. Part of me hoped she wouldn't come. Part of me wondered if God knew what He was asking.

She came.

At the reception, Sister Johnson approached with trembling hands and tear-filled eyes. The years had changed her, softened her somehow. "I never apologized for what I did to you," she whispered, her voice breaking. "I was battling severe depression and made terrible decisions. I wasn't well. I hurt you when you needed help. Will you forgive me?"

In that moment, I realized something profound. Forgiveness had already taken root in me the moment I obeyed God's whisper. Her apology brought healing and closure, but my freedom had never depended on it. The walls were already down before she ever said a word. I had been free for months without even realizing it.

That's the mystery of obedient forgiveness; it liberates the forgiver long before the offender ever acknowledges the offense.

The Four R's: A Roadmap to Freedom

Through my journey, and through helping others navigate their own paths toward forgiveness, I have found that forgiveness follows four stages. Think of them as guideposts on the road from bondage to freedom.

1. Recognition: See the Wound Clearly

Do not minimize it. Jesus did not pretend the cross did not hurt. He cried out in agony, sweat blood in the garden, and expressed the full weight of His suffering. Healthy forgiveness begins with honest acknowledgment.

Write down exactly what happened and how it affected you. Be specific. Name the emotions: betrayal, humiliation, fear, and anger. List the consequences: financial loss, damaged relationships, shattered trust. Bring it to God in raw, unfiltered honesty. He can handle your pain. He already knows the depth of it anyway.

Recognition says, "This happened. It was wrong. It hurt me. And I'm not pretending it didn't."

2. Release: Place It in God's Hands

Forgiveness is a choice, not a feeling. You may not feel forgiving, and that's okay. You choose to forgive anyway, trusting that the feelings will eventually follow the decision.

Release does not mean "it did not matter." It means "I will not carry it anymore." It means you're transferring the weight from your shoulders to God's hands, where it belongs.

Prayer: "God, I choose to release [name] and [offense] into Your hands. I will not be their judge, jury, or executioner. I trust You to handle this justly. I lay down the burden of bitterness and pick up Your gift of peace."

This prayer may need to be repeated daily, even hourly at first. Forgiveness is often a series of choices, not a single decision.

3. Restoration: Rebuild What Is Possible

Here's a crucial truth many miss: Forgiveness does not always mean reconciliation. Some relationships can be restored, others require healthy boundaries. Forgiveness is a gift you give. Reconciliation is a process that requires both parties.

You can forgive someone and still maintain distance. You can release bitterness while refusing to re-enter a toxic dynamic. Forgiveness opens your heart. Wisdom protects it.

Ask yourself: Is this relationship safe to restore? Has genuine change occurred? Are there patterns of repeated harm? Forgiveness is mandatory. Reconciliation is conditional. Know the difference.

4. Redemption: Let God Use Your Pain

God is a master at turning messes into messages and tests into testimonies. Every wound in your story has the potential to become a ministry to someone else walking a similar path.

Share your story when the time is right. What once hurt you can now heal someone else. Your breakthrough becomes their roadmap. Your victory becomes their hope.

Redemption doesn't erase what happened, but it ensures it wasn't wasted. God wastes nothing, not even your deepest pain.

The Sister Johnson Epilogue

Later, I learned Sister Johnson's eviction was not only about me. She was in the grip of untreated depression that led to destructive choices affecting multiple areas of her life. With counseling and pastoral care, she eventually found healing and now helps others battling mental health and faith struggles.

Had I clung to unforgiveness, I would have missed seeing the redemption God was writing in both of our lives. Both of us had been prisoners. She was bound by depression, and I was bound by unforgiveness. Freedom came when we both chose healing over holding on.

Today, Sister Johnson and I are not just reconciled, we're allies in ministry. The woman I once wanted excluded from my wedding now prays for my marriage. The betrayal that nearly destroyed my faith became the foundation for a testimony that has encouraged countless others.

That's what redemption looks like. God doesn't just repair broken things. He repurposes them into something stronger than they were before.

The Forgiveness Walk: A Tool for Your Journey

As you read this, you may be asking, "How do I begin?" Forgiveness can feel overwhelming, especially when the hurt runs deep. I have developed a simple tool called **The Forgiveness Walk** to help you walk step by step toward freedom.

1. **Prepare Your Heart**

   Find a quiet space and invite God into the moment. Ask Him to reveal who or what you need to forgive.

2. **Name the Wound**

   Write down exactly what happened. Do not minimize it or make excuses for it. Truth brings light, and light brings healing.

3. **Release the Burden**

   Speak the words aloud: "God, I release this person and this pain into Your hands." If emotions rise, let them. Healing often begins with tears.

4. **Pray the Blessing**

   Ask God to bless the one who hurt you. This step is not about agreement with what they did. It is about freeing your heart from the weight of bitterness.

5. **Receive God's Peace**

   Sit in stillness and let His peace fill the space that pain once occupied. You may not feel it immediately, but peace always follows obedience.

Forgiveness is not a single event. It is a journey. Sometimes you may have to repeat these steps again until the wound no longer defines you. Each time you choose forgiveness, the chains lose more of their power.

The world teaches that holding on gives you control. Heaven teaches that letting go gives you freedom. When you forgive, heaven takes notice. The chains fall. The heart heals. And the story that once caused you pain becomes the testimony that sets someone else free.

Reflection Questions

- Which of the Five Walls resonates most with you right now? What would your life look like if that wall came down?
- Which of the Four R's feels most challenging? What makes it difficult? What would it take to move forward?
- Is there someone you need to forgive but have been waiting for an apology that may never come? What would change if you forgave them anyway?

Closing Thought

The same God who gave you the strength to survive the wound can give you the power to transcend it. Your prison has no lock that His grace cannot open. Your walls have no height that His love cannot scale. No offense is too great for His mercy to cover, no betrayal too deep for His grace to reach.

Today, choose to embrace a fresh start. Choose the liberation that comes when you lay down the burden you were never meant to carry. Choose freedom over fairness, peace over revenge, and watch what God can do with a heart that trusts Him enough to forgive.

The key to your prison is in your hand. It always has been. It's called forgiveness.

Chapter Three

Assess - Discovering Your Hidden Treasure

From Fear to Discovery

In Chapter One, we unmasked fear and saw how it disguises itself as perfectionism, procrastination, or people-pleasing. Recognizing those masks was our first step toward freedom. In Chapter Two, we learned that forgiveness liberates us from the chains of our past, freeing us to move forward unencumbered by bitterness.

But recognition and release alone are not enough. Once we have faced fear and embraced forgiveness, we must take the next step: discovering the treasures God has already placed within us.

Fear does not only keep us from stepping into our future. It blinds us to what we already carry. When we are consumed with what we lack, paralyzed by what might go wrong, or fixated on our inadequacies, we fail to see the gifts and strengths God has entrusted to us. Fear is a master of misdirection, always pointing our attention toward empty spaces while hiding the full shelves right in front of us.

The same courage that helped us face our fears and release our hurts will help us uncover our treasures. This is the journey from deficit thinking to abundance awareness, from "I have nothing" to "Look what God has given me."

When We Think We Have Nothing

In 2 Kings 4, a widow faced her darkest fears. Her husband had died, debts were mounting, and creditors threatened to enslave her sons. This wasn't just financial pressure, this was the potential loss of everything she had left. Her children, her only remaining treasure, were about to be torn from her arms to pay debts she couldn't satisfy.

Desperate, she cried out to the prophet Elisha. He asked her a simple question, yet it was loaded with divine intention: "What do you have in your house?"

Her reply carried the weight of defeat: "Nothing at all, except a small jar of oil."

Hear the resignation in her voice. Notice how quickly she dismissed what she did have. "Nothing at all", as if the oil didn't count, as if it was too insignificant to mention, as if God couldn't possibly use something so small.

How often do we say the same? Fear teaches us to focus on what is missing. It whispers that our skills are not valuable, our experiences are not useful, and our passions are not practical. We become experts at dismissing our assets with that deadly word: "except."

"I have nothing, except a little creativity." "I have nothing, except some experience with technology." "I have nothing, except this painful story."

Yet the very "except" she dismissed became the instrument of her miracle. When she began pouring the oil, it flowed until every jar was filled, every debt was paid, and her family's future was secured. What she thought was worthless turned out to be more than enough. The oil kept flowing as long as she kept pouring, supernatural supply meeting natural obedience.

The same hands that trembled with fear became the hands that poured out the miracle. Your trembling hands can do the same.

Fear Blinds Our Vision

Research from Harvard reveals that most professionals feel underutilized, while simultaneously believing they lack the skills to pursue their dreams. This paradox shows how fear blinds us. We're caught in a strange contradiction, feeling like we're wasting our potential while also believing we don't have enough potential to pursue what matters.

We become experts at cataloging our deficits while remaining blind to our assets. We can list our weaknesses in alphabetical order, but struggle to name three genuine strengths. We remember every failure in vivid detail, yet we dismiss our successes as mere luck or timing.

Fear narrows our vision like blinders on a horse. We see only what we lack, only the gaps, only the missing pieces. But God invites us to lift our eyes and notice what He has already placed in our lives. He asks us the same question. He asked the widow: "What do you have?"

Not what you wish you had. Not what others have. What do *you* have, right now, in your house, in your hands, in your story?

A Modern Story of Discovery

Scott Harrison's journey reflects this same truth. For years, he lived a life of indulgence as a nightclub promoter in New York City. On the surface, he seemed to have everything, money, status, connections, excitement. Yet inside he felt empty, hollowed out by a lifestyle that promised fulfillment but delivered only hangovers and regret.

When he finally stepped away from that world, he had no money, no possessions of value, and no clear direction. He was 28 years old and starting over from scratch. By the world's standards, he had nothing.

But Scott assessed what he *did* have. He carried organizational skills honed from managing complex events. He possessed a talent for storytelling and creating compelling experiences. He had a passion to help people in need that had been awakened during a season serving on a hospital ship in West Africa. With those simple gifts, gifts he almost dismissed as "nothing at all," he founded charity: water, a non-profit committed to bringing clean drinking water to communities around the world.

What began with one man's "small jar of oil" has now brought clean water to over 17 million people in more than 29 countries. His organization has raised over $740 million, not through traditional charity tactics, but through the very storytelling and organizational gifts Scott once used to promote nightclubs.

Scott's story reminds us that what seems small in our hands can become a miracle in God's. When we stop saying "nothing at all" and begin to pour out what we already have, God multiplies it beyond anything we could imagine. Your past isn't wasted. Your skills aren't irrelevant. Your experiences aren't accidents. They're all oil in the jar, waiting to be poured.

Our Shared Journey

I have experienced this truth in my own journey. When I first stepped into prison ministry more than twenty years ago, I felt completely unqualified. Fear kept saying, "You do not have the right degree. You do not have the credentials. Who do you think you are? These men need real counselors, trained chaplains, people with theological education. What do you have to offer?"

All I carried was a Bible, a testimony of God's grace, and a willingness to listen. By fear's measure, that was nothing at all. By the world's standards, I was underqualified and underprepared. But as I poured out what I had, God did the multiplying.

One of the men I met inside, Robert, once told me, "You are the first person who talks to us like we are still human beings capable of change." His words shattered something in me. I realized that what I thought was "nothing" was actually everything these men needed to be seen, to be heard, to be reminded they were made in God's image, despite their mistakes.

Years later, I was standing in worship at my local church when a young man approached me. With a smile, he said, "I am not sure if you remember me, but I am a former inmate from Maplehurst Correctional Complex." Maplehurst is one of the prisons where I have led outreach programs for over two decades.

My mind raced, trying to place him. The transformation was so complete I couldn't reconcile this confident, well-dressed man with anyone I remembered from behind bars.

He went on, "The words and messages of love that you shared with me and my fellow inmates changed my life." He then introduced me to his wife, his hand resting protectively on her shoulder. With joy in his voice, he explained that he had found steady employment, that he and his wife were saving to buy a home, and that they were building a future together. They were expecting their first child.

Due to security guidelines, we rarely see inmates again after their release. So to stand face-to-face with a young man who had once been behind bars, now walking in freedom, stability, and faith, now about to become a father, was deeply moving. I could not stop thanking God for the transformation that only Jesus could bring.

In that moment, I was reminded again that what we think is "nothing at all" can change lives when we pour it out in obedience. I could not take credit for his transformation. That was the work of Christ. But God allowed me to play a part simply by offering what I had. He didn't need my credentials. He needed my obedience.

Not long after, the Holy Spirit gave me an even deeper understanding of this truth. In prayer, I sensed Him walking me through the aisles of a grocery store, carefully scanning each shelf of my life. It felt as though He was pointing out the hidden treasures I had overlooked: twenty years of prison outreach that had given me resilience and compassion, decades in project management that had sharpened leadership and vision, personal struggles that had shaped empathy and perseverance, a testimony of God's faithfulness through seasons of waiting, and skills in communication I had developed but never fully valued. I realized I had been living like the widow, saying, "Nothing at all," while God was showing me that my shelves were already stocked with treasures prepared for His purposes. Every experience, even the painful ones, had been adding oil to my jar. Nothing was wasted. Nothing was accidental.

Steps to Assess Your Treasure: The GIFT Approach

To help us recognize what God has already given, I use the word GIFT as a simple guide. This framework has helped me and countless others move from deficit thinking to abundance awareness.

Gather: Begin by listing what we already have.

Write down our skills, our experiences, our perspectives, and our passions. Nothing is too small to include. Don't edit yourself. Don't dismiss anything as "too ordinary" or "not special enough."

Include technical skills (Can you use Excel? Write clearly? Fix things? Organize events?), relational skills (Are you a good listener? Peacemaker? Encourager?), experiential wisdom (Have you overcome addiction? Navigated loss? Raised children? Managed finances through difficulty?), and passionate interests (What topics make you come alive? What injustices stir you? What brings you joy?).

This isn't about ego or pride. It's about honest inventory. You're not bragging, you're accounting for what God has deposited in your life.

Identify: Notice what we tend to dismiss.

Ask: What do I say "nothing at all, except" about in my own life? Those overlooked areas may hold our greatest potential. Pay attention to what you minimize, what you apologize for, and what you think doesn't count.

Sometimes our most valuable treasure is hiding in plain sight, disguised as something ordinary. The widow's oil was just a household supply until God multiplied it. Your "just" might be your miracle: "I'm just a good listener." "I just know how to code." "I just survived cancer." "I just understand what it's like to be overlooked."

That "just" is God's starting point.

Focus: Seek God's perspective.

Pray, "Holy Spirit, show us what You see in us." God's perspective is radically different from ours. We see limitations; He sees potential. We see failures; He sees lessons learned. We see ordinary; He sees raw material for miracles.

Ask trusted friends when they have seen us at our best. Sometimes others see clearly what we cannot. They notice when our eyes light up, when we're in our element, when we operate with unusual grace and effectiveness. Their observations can reveal blind spots in our self-awareness.

Ask specifically: "When have you seen me most alive? What do you think I'm good at? What do you come to me for?" Their answers may surprise you and point to treasures you've been taking for granted.

Trust: Take the step of pouring it out.

The widow's miracle did not come until she began to pour. She could have stared at that jar of oil forever, wishing it were more, doubting it would work, wondering if Elisha's instructions made sense. But nothing happened until she acted.

Our treasures multiply when we offer them, even when they feel small. Start where you are, with what you have. Offer your "except" to God and watch what He does with it.

The multiplication happens in the pouring, not in the planning.

From Ordinary to Overflow

The miracle of multiplication begins with what seems ordinary. Leadership expert John Maxwell says, "Success is when I add value to myself. Significance is when I add value to others."

Our overlooked "except" may be a hidden ability, a painful lesson, or a quiet passion. Yet when offered in obedience, God multiplies it for His purposes. He takes the ordinary and makes it extraordinary, not by changing its nature, but by changing its scale and impact.

We may use tools like StrengthsFinder, Myers-Briggs, or personality assessments to gain insight, and these can be helpful. But ultimately, God is the one who defines our calling. When He looks at us, He does not see "nothing." He sees preparation. He sees raw materials. He sees treasure.

Every experience you've had, good and bad, has been adding to your jar. Every lesson learned, every hardship survived, every skill developed, every relationship navigated. It's all oil. The question is: will you pour it out?

The widow discovered abundance when she stopped saying "nothing at all" and started pouring. She didn't wait until she felt confident. She didn't wait until she had more.

She didn't wait until the circumstances made sense. She simply obeyed with what she had.

The same is true for us. Your miracle is waiting on the other side of your obedience.

The Courage to See What God Sees

Sometimes the hardest part of discovering your hidden treasure is believing it is really there. We grow accustomed to seeing only what is broken, missing, or insufficient. Our inner dialogue often sounds like the widow's: "Nothing at all, except…" But heaven sees something entirely different.

When God looks at you, He does not see lack. He sees potential waiting to be poured. Every gift, every lesson, every scar, and every success becomes part of your divine inventory. What you may call ordinary, God calls essential. The enemy's goal is to keep your vision small so that you never recognize what is already in your hands.

Many of us spend our energy trying to find a new assignment instead of assessing what God has already entrusted to us. The truth is, your next breakthrough is often hidden inside your current obedience. The small thing you keep overlooking may be the very oil that God intends to multiply.

During one season of prayer, I sensed the Lord asking, "What are you doing with what you already have?" It was not a question of shame but of invitation. As I listed the things I had dismissed as insignificant, I realized how much I had underestimated His provision. The conversations I had with inmates. The skills I had gained in leadership. The lessons I had learned through hardship. Each one was a treasure disguised as experience.

It is easy to wait for a "big moment," but most miracles begin with small steps. God rarely asks us to start with what we do not have. He invites us to begin with what is already in our house.

The Treasure Map: A Tool for Discovery

To help uncover these hidden treasures, I use a simple tool called **The Treasure Map**. It is a prayerful exercise designed to help you assess what God has already placed within you.

1. **Pray for Clarity**

    Begin by inviting the Holy Spirit to guide your thoughts. Ask Him to reveal what gifts, experiences, and passions He has already given you.

2. **List Your Jars of Oil**

    Write down every ability, skill, relationship, or story that has shaped your life. Include things that seem too small to matter. God loves to multiply the small.

3. **Connect the Dots**

Look for patterns between your experiences and your passions. What burdens stir your heart? What kind of problems do you naturally feel drawn to solve? Often, your calling is connected to your compassion.

4. **Offer It Back to God**

Once you see what you carry, pray, "Lord, I offer this to You. Use it however You will." This moment of surrender turns assessment into alignment.

5. **Act in Faith**

Take one step toward using what you have discovered. Send that message. Volunteer your skill. Share your testimony. Pour the oil.

When you begin to walk this path, you will realize that discovery and obedience are deeply connected. The more you pour, the more God reveals. You may not feel qualified, but God never calls the qualified; He qualifies those who are willing to pour.

The same God who filled the widow's jars is still at work today. He is not asking for what you do not have. He is asking for what is already in your house. Your "small jar of oil" may just be the beginning of someone else's miracle.

So, gather your courage, open your eyes, and assess what God has already placed within you. The treasure is not hidden from you. It is hidden in you, waiting for you to pour it out in faith.

Reflection Prompt:

Take fifteen minutes this week to create your own Treasure Map. Write down your "jars of oil," no matter how small they seem. Ask God to show you how He can use them for His glory.

The Bridge Forward

The same God who gave the widow oil to pour and courage to believe has placed treasures within us, too. But there is one barrier that can keep the jar sealed: the lies we believe about ourselves and the words spoken over us by those who couldn't see our value.

Sometimes the greatest obstacle to discovering and pouring out our gifts is the bitterness we carry toward those who once told us, "You have nothing." Or the shame we feel from times we tried to pour and the oil didn't flow the way we expected. Or the fear that what we have isn't enough.

But here's the truth: what God has placed in you is enough. Not because you're extraordinary, but because He is. Not because your jar is full, but because His supply is endless. Not because you have it all figured out, but because He knows exactly how to multiply what you offer.

Your treasure is real, your "except" matters. Your oil is ready to flow.

The only question remaining is: will you pour?

The Bridge to Forgiveness

The same God who gave the widow oil to pour and courage to believe has placed treasures within us, too. But there is one barrier that can keep the jar sealed: unforgiveness. Sometimes the greatest obstacle to discovering and pouring out our gifts is the bitterness we carry toward those who once told us, "You have nothing." That is why our next step is so important. In Chapter Three, we will discover how forgiveness liberates us from the invisible prisons of resentment and frees us to fully embrace the treasures God has placed in us.

The Courage to Begin Again

Choosing to begin is not a one-time decision. It is a choice we make again and again, especially when setbacks come. The truth is, every calling faces resistance. Every dream encounters discouragement. But courage is not the absence of fear; it is the decision to move forward despite it.

I have learned that beginnings are rarely glamorous. They are often hidden, quiet, and uncomfortable. You may begin with trembling hands or uncertain steps, yet heaven celebrates that moment of obedience. God is not impressed by perfection. He is moved by willingness.

There were seasons when I thought I had already begun, only to realize I was still standing at the edge of fear, waiting for conditions to be perfect. But perfect conditions never come. The longer you wait for the wind to calm, the longer your sails remain empty. The miracle of movement begins when you lift your anchor and trust God with the direction of your journey.

Every story of transformation begins with a simple yes. That, yes, may sound small, but it has the power to rewrite your entire future. When Moses said yes, a nation was freed. When Peter said yes, the church was born. When Mary said yes, salvation entered the world. Heaven moves when you do.

The Courage Compass: A Tool for Movement

To help you take that first step, I created something I call **The Courage Compass**. It is a simple guide to help you move from hesitation to action, one faithful decision at a time.

1. **Center Your Heart**

   Begin with prayer. Ask God to calm your mind and remind you of His presence. Fear loses its grip when you remember who walks with you.

2. **Clarify Your Direction**

   Write down what God has placed in your heart to begin. It could be a project, a ministry, a phone call, or a difficult conversation. Be specific. Clarity turns confusion into courage.

3. **Count the Cost Honestly**

   Every act of obedience requires something. Time, humility, discipline, or change. Write down what it will cost and offer it to God. Courage grows in the soil of surrender.

4. **Commit to a Step**

   Choose one tangible action you can take within the next twenty-four hours. Send the message, open the notebook, schedule the meeting, or begin the plan. Action breaks the grip of fear.

5. **Celebrate Progress**

   Each step you take is sacred. Heaven rejoices over movement because movement means trust. Take time to thank God for every small victory and let gratitude build momentum for the next step.

As you use this tool, remember that courage is not a feeling you wait for; it is a posture you choose. The enemy will always tempt you with tomorrow, but faith calls you to act today. Every time you choose obedience over delay, you strengthen the muscle of courage.

There will be days when progress feels invisible and steps feel uncertain. On those days, remind yourself that the seed of greatness always begins underground. The unseen work of today prepares the visible harvest of tomorrow. God delights in your first steps, no matter how small they may seem.

You are not waiting for courage to find you. Courage is waiting for you to begin.

Reflection Prompt:

Ask yourself, "What is one thing I can start today that I have been postponing?" Write it down, pray over it, and take your first step. Remember, obedience always invites God's provision.

Chapter Four

Choose - The Courage to Begin

The Lie of Tomorrow

One of fear's most seductive lies is that time is infinite. It whispers, "Tomorrow I will forgive. Tomorrow I will start my business venture. Tomorrow I will step into my calling." But tomorrow is a mirage that never arrives. It's always one day away, perpetually out of reach, like chasing the horizon.

Procrastination disguises itself as patience, but it is resistance in disguise. It wears the mask of wisdom, speaking in reasonable tones about timing and readiness. It may look harmless, but it quietly steals the life you are meant to live. Tomorrow is the thief of destiny, robbing you of opportunities that only exist today. The door that stands open before you now may be closed when "tomorrow" finally comes.

Waiting feels safe, but too often it is where dreams go to die. There's comfort in the familiar prison of "not yet," a strange security in perpetual preparation that never graduates to action.

The Israelites learned this in the wilderness. What should have been an eleven-day journey to the Promised Land stretched into forty years of circles. Not because God lacked power, but because His people delayed obedience. They stood at the border of promise and said, "Not yet. We're not ready. The obstacles are too great. Tomorrow we'll be more prepared."

A whole generation died in the desert, never tasting the promise within reach. They could see it from the mountaintop, the land flowing with milk and honey, but fear convinced them to wait. And wait. And wait. Until waiting became their entire existence, and the promise became a memory instead of a reality.

Delay cost them dearly. Delay costs you too.

Tomorrow always sounds like wisdom. It promises that later you will have more courage, better circumstances, and clearer direction. It assures you that future-you will be braver, more qualified, more prepared. But tomorrow is an illusion that keeps you chained to hesitation, a prison with invisible bars that feels like a waiting room.

The Israelites' tragedy still echoes today. People with vision, potential, and calling lose years circling in comfort rather than stepping into promise. The desert of "not yet" has buried countless dreams, books never written, businesses never launched, ministries never started, relationships never pursued, forgiveness never offered.

As John Maxwell says, "You don't overcome challenges by making them smaller but by making yourself bigger." You do not grow by waiting for courage. You grow when you choose to act in faith, even while fear trembles in the background. Courage isn't the absence of fear; it's the decision to move forward while fear screams for you to stay put.

The Grace of Small Beginnings

The liberating truth is this: God does not require perfection before progress. He simply asks for a beginning. He doesn't need your polished performance; He wants your willing participation.

Zechariah 4:10 reminds you, "Do not despise these small beginnings, for the Lord rejoices to see the work begin." That shaky, awkward first step may feel too small to matter, but small beginnings carry supernatural weight when you choose to step forward in obedience. God doesn't measure your first step by its size but by its direction.

I experienced this in a very personal way. For years, I told myself the lie of "someday." I convinced myself I needed more education, more experience, and more confidence before I could write this book. Fear disguised itself as prudence, whispering that waiting was wise while action was reckless. "You need another degree first," it said. "You need to read more books. You need to become a better writer. You need to have all the answers before you dare put pen to paper."

But one Tuesday morning, sitting in my office with a cup of coffee, staring at the blinking cursor on my laptop screen, I felt the weight of a choice. The silence pressed in, heavy and expectant. My hands trembled. My chest felt tight. My mind whispered, "Who do you think you are to write this? Who will read it? What if you fail publicly?"

Then came the quiet nudge of the Spirit: *Begin.*

It was not a loud command but a steady whisper that cut through the noise of fear. It didn't promise success or guarantee an audience. It simply invited obedience. My heart pounded as I typed the first sentence. It was awkward. It felt clumsy. I deleted it and tried again. Still imperfect. But it was a beginning.

And the moment I chose to move, God met me in motion. Ideas began to flow like water from a previously blocked pipe. Connections came to mind. Scriptures I'd read years ago suddenly had new relevance. Courage slowly replaced hesitation, not because fear disappeared, but because momentum overpowered it.

What once seemed impossible suddenly became inevitable. The book you're holding right now is proof that

God honors the courage to begin, even when that beginning feels small and insufficient.

Glimpses of Leadership

I can still remember when one of my managers told me, "You have glimpses of leadership." At the time, I did not see myself that way. I was still learning, still stumbling, and still second-guessing myself. The word "glimpses" felt almost like a consolation prize, not quite there yet, but showing potential. It was encouraging and discouraging at the same time.

But those words stayed with me, planted like a seed waiting for the right conditions to grow.

Even though I doubted myself, I chose to step into small opportunities. I initiated projects, led conversations, and launched ideas at work, all while battling fear and feeling like I had nothing valuable to add in the executive room. My heart often pounded in meetings, and I wondered if others noticed my insecurities. Could they hear the tremor in my voice? Did they see my hands shaking as I presented? Was my imposter syndrome written across my face?

Then came a moment I will never forget. I was in a team meeting with our Project Vice President, who was visiting from out of town. At that point, my role was mostly administrative. I took minutes for my manager and rarely spoke in those high-level discussions. I was there to observe and document, not to contribute. But this meeting was different.

The leaders were going back and forth on what direction the project should take. Voices grew louder, positions became entrenched, and the tension in the room was palpable. Then the Vice President did something unexpected. He turned to me, the quietest person in the room, the one taking notes in the corner, and asked, "Kirk, you have been very quiet. What are your thoughts? How should we proceed?"

The room fell silent. All eyes turned to me. My pulse quickened. This was my wilderness moment, I could retreat into "I'm just here to take notes," or I could step into the opportunity fear told me I wasn't ready for.

I was caught off guard, but I shared honestly and carefully. I laid out what I'd been observing, offered a perspective that bridged the competing viewpoints, and suggested a path forward. When I finished, there was a pause. Then nods. Then agreement.

After the meeting, the Vice President pulled me aside and said he wanted me to chair those meetings going forward. Those meetings I'd been attending silently for months were now mine to lead. That small moment of courage led to greater responsibility, doors opening I hadn't even known existed.

A few years later, that same Vice President honored me with the Company's CEO Award, which included $10,000 in company stock. What began as a terrified response to an unexpected question became recognized leadership and tangible reward.

I share this example not to boast, but to highlight how small beginnings can grow when you choose to step forward. What began as a quiet voice in a meeting became recognized leadership. It reminded me that God often plants seeds of purpose in you that others see before you do. That manager who saw "glimpses" was seeing what God was cultivating, even when I was blind to it.

When you choose to step forward, even in fear, He multiplies your efforts in ways you could never arrange for yourself. He opens doors you didn't knock on, creates opportunities you didn't apply for, and positions you for influence you didn't campaign for.

A decade later, I crossed paths with that same manager who once told me I had glimpses of leadership. By then, I was serving as a Senior Program Manager, leading complex projects and mentoring others. After a few months of working together again, he said something that brought my journey full circle: "I am so pleased to see your maturity into a strong leader."

From "glimpses" to "strong leader." That transformation didn't happen because I waited until I felt ready. It happened because I chose to begin right where I was.

That full-circle moment showed me that growth comes not from waiting until you feel ready, but from choosing to begin right where you are. The beginning may feel small and uncertain, but it is the only way to reach maturity. You cannot arrive at mastery without first embracing the awkwardness of being a beginner.

The Purposeful Pause

Not all waiting is wasted. Sometimes, what feels like a delay is actually divine preparation. This is a critical distinction that fear doesn't want you to understand, because if you can tell the difference between God's preparation and fear's paralysis, you become dangerous to the kingdom of darkness.

David was anointed king as a boy but did not wear the crown until years later. Those hidden years weren't wasted, they were the training ground where a shepherd became a warrior, where a musician became a psalmist, where a fugitive became a king. In caves and wilderness, God was developing the character that could handle the crown.

Joseph spent over a decade between pit, prison, and palace. What looked like wasted years were actually preparing him to save nations. Every injustice, every false accusation, every forgotten promise was shaping a man who could wield power without abusing it, who could forgive brothers who betrayed him, who could see God's hand even in the darkest dungeons.

Waiting with purpose is not passive. It is a season to sharpen your skills, deepen your character, and prepare for doors not yet open. It's studying while the door is closed so you're ready when it opens. It's building relationships, gaining experience, and developing discipline.

The danger comes when waiting shifts from purposeful to paralyzing. Fear-driven delay resembles endless planning without action, hoping without movement, and praying without obedience. It looks like perpetual preparation that never graduates to participation. It sounds like "I'm waiting on God" when God has been waiting on you.

The key difference is activity. Purposeful waiting builds. Fearful waiting buries. Purposeful waiting says, "The door isn't open yet, so I'm preparing for when it does." Fearful waiting says, "I hope the door never opens because I'm terrified of what's on the other side."

C. S. Lewis captured this beautifully: "You can't go back and change the beginning, but you can start where you are and change the ending." Your past doesn't define your future. Your beginning doesn't determine your conclusion. Today is your turning point if you choose to make it so.

The Science of Momentum

Stanford research confirms what Scripture has long revealed: motivation does not create action; action creates motivation. We've been told the opposite our entire lives, that we need to feel motivated before we act. But the truth is backward from what we've believed.

Small steps trigger dopamine, fueling further progress. Your brain rewards action with feel-good chemicals that make the next action easier. Scientists call it a "momentum loop." The Bible calls it faithful stewardship. Jesus taught it in the parable of talents: to those who use what they have, more is given.

James 1:22 says, "Be doers of the word, and not hearers only." Action fuels transformation. Hearing alone changes nothing. Planning alone accomplishes nothing. Only doing creates the momentum that carries you forward.

The smallest motion forward can generate supernatural momentum. The first page leads to the first chapter. The first conversation leads to the first partnership. The first investment leads to the first return. But nothing happens until something moves.

This is why the hardest part is not writing the book, launching the business, or making the call. The hardest part is choosing to start. But once you move, motion becomes your ally, carrying you further than you imagined. Inertia works both ways, objects at rest stay at rest, but objects in motion stay in motion.

A Story of Choosing Today

Christine Caine is a modern example of the power of choosing to begin. For years she struggled with insecurity, believing she was unqualified to make a global impact. Abandoned as an infant, abused as a child, told she would never amount to anything, her beginning didn't suggest a future of influence.

But when confronted with the reality of human trafficking, she chose to act. She could have said, "I'm not qualified. I don't have the resources. Someone more important should handle this." Instead, she took one step, then another, then another.

What began as one small step of obedience grew into A21, a global organization now fighting slavery in multiple countries around the world. They've rescued thousands, prosecuted traffickers, and prevented countless others from falling into exploitation. Christine often says, "God is not waiting for you to feel ready. He is waiting for you to be willing."

Her story reminds you that God can multiply one courageous step into something that transforms lives and nations when you choose to step forward. Your beginning doesn't have to be impressive; it just has to be obedient.

Your Crossroads Moment

Right now, you may find yourself in a similar place. A blank page waiting for your words. An idea stirring that refuses to stay quiet. A dream pressing against your heart, asking for permission to live. A conversation you know you need to have. A forgiveness you know you need to offer. A risk you know you need to take.

Moses led despite his stutter. Gideon fought despite his fear. David advanced despite his youth. Christine Caine launched a global ministry despite her insecurities. I finally wrote this book despite my hesitation. And along the way, people saw glimpses of leadership in me even when I could not see it in myself. Years later, that glimpse had grown into maturity because I chose to begin where I was.

The question is not whether you are ready. The question is whether you will choose to start. God has never required readiness, only willingness. He doesn't need your ability; He needs your availability.

Proverbs 27:1 warns: "Do not boast about tomorrow, for you do not know what a day may bring." Tomorrow is not promised. The opportunity you see today may not be there tomorrow. The person you need to forgive may not be here tomorrow. The dream burning in your heart may fade if you don't fan the flame today.

Today is all you have. Tomorrow is an illusion. Yesterday is history. This moment, right now, is your point of power.

Final Word

The world is not waiting for your perfection. It is waiting for your beginning. Every journey of significance begins not with flawless execution but with the courage to choose today.

Choosing to begin, even in fear, is the first act of courage that unlocks your destiny. It's the key that fits the lock on your future. And that key has been in your hand all along, waiting for you to use it.

Chapter Five

Hope – The Power to Move Forward

We have walked an incredible journey together. You unmasked fear and stripped away its lies in Chapter One, recognizing that the voice telling you "you are not enough" was never God's voice. You broke the chains of unforgiveness in Chapter Two, embracing the freedom that comes when you release what was never yours to carry. You discovered the treasure God already placed within you in Chapter Three, assessing your unique abilities and destiny with fresh eyes. You took your first steps in Chapter Four, choosing courage over comfort and action over analysis.

And now, as we reach the summit of our R.E.A.C.H. framework, the moment of hope has arrived.

Everything so far has been preparation. This is the chapter where the oil begins to pour. This is where the world feels the weight of your purpose. But here is what I need you to understand as we stand at this threshold: **hope is not the happy ending to your transformation story. Hope is the fuel that will power you through everything that comes next.**

Why Hope Matters

Maya Angelou once said, *"Hope and fear cannot occupy the same space. Invite one to stay."*

Hope is not naive optimism or wishful thinking. Biblical hope is a **confident expectation rooted in the unchanging character of God.** It is the anchor that steadies you when storms crash against your destiny.

Releasing your potential and stepping into your purpose doesn't mean the battles are over. In many ways, it means they are just beginning. But you'll face them differently now, because hope changes everything.

Hope gives you the divine advantage of perspective. It allows you to see beyond what is happening to what God is forming. It whispers to your heart, *"This is not where your story ends."*

The apostle Paul understood this deeply. In **2 Corinthians 4:8–9**, he wrote:

"We are hard pressed on every side, but not crushed; perplexed, but not in despair; persecuted, but not abandoned; struck down, but not destroyed."

Hope allowed Paul to endure persecution, loss, and hardship while still carrying his assignment to completion. He was not sustained by comfort; he was sustained by confidence, the confidence that God's promises outlast pain.

The Reality of Resistance

Let's be honest: the closer you get to destiny, the greater the resistance. Opposition does not decrease with progress; it often multiplies.

There will be days when your progress feels invisible. Critics will question your motives. Circumstances will conspire to test your resolve. Fear will reappear wearing new disguises. Forgiveness will be tested by fresh wounds. Your commitment to act will be challenged by new forms of delay.

This is not pessimism; it is **preparation**. Resistance is proof that you are on the right path.

Paul knew this intimately. He wasn't sugarcoating the journey; he was showing us that hardship doesn't define the faithful, **hope does**. The world may see your scars, but God sees your story. The very pressure that tries to break you becomes the tool that shapes your endurance.

A Story of Hope

Consider Malala Yousafzai, the Pakistani girl who was shot in the head by extremists simply for going to school. By every measure, her story could have ended there, silenced by violence. Yet Malala's hope refused to die. She recovered and used her voice to advocate for girls' education around the world. In 2014, at just seventeen years old, she became the youngest Nobel Peace Prize laureate.

Malala's story shows us what hope can do. Hope does not erase tragedy; it **transforms it into testimony.** Hope does not deny suffering; it insists that suffering will not have the final word.

And you have that same power within you. Every wound can become a window through which God's light shines brighter. Every setback can become a setup for a greater revelation of His strength in your weakness. Hope takes what was meant to bury you and turns it into the soil where your faith grows deeper roots.

What Hope Really Does

Hope is what separates those who start from those who finish. It turns enthusiasm into endurance and transforms small beginnings into lasting impact.

Hebrews 6:19 calls hope "an anchor for the soul, firm and secure." Notice it doesn't say hope stops the storm; it says hope steadies you through it.

Here's what hope accomplishes in those released for purpose:

- **Hope reframes failure.** Setbacks are not the end; they become lessons and redirections in God's hands.

- **Hope sustains vision.** When circumstances contradict your destiny, hope clings to God's promises longer than logic thinks reasonable.
- **Hope fuels perseverance.** While others quit when the journey grows hard, hope whispers, *"Keep going, the breakthrough is near."*
- **Hope multiplies impact.** In a world drowning in despair, those who live with hope shine as lighthouses guiding others home.

C.S. Lewis captured this beautifully when he wrote, *"We are never too old to set another goal or to dream a new dream."*

Hope reminds us that it is never too late, never too broken, never too impossible.

Hope in an Age of Uncertainty

Our generation is living through turbulence, economic instability, social division, technological disruption, and global crises. Fear says, *"This is the end."* But hope says, *"This is the beginning."*

Dr. Martin Seligman, known as the father of positive psychology, has warned of an "epidemic of hopelessness" sweeping across cultures. Yet this is exactly why your hope matters more than ever.

When you choose to live with hope, you become a living contradiction to despair. You become evidence that faith still works, that love still wins, and that God still reigns.

Your destiny is not just about you. Hope makes you a **carrier of light** for others still searching in the dark. When you walk in hope, your life becomes a message, not just of survival, but of resurrection.

So, stand tall. Lift your eyes again. The same God who began this work in you will carry it to completion. The journey doesn't end here, it's only beginning.

Because when hope lives in you, you are unstoppable.

The Practice of Hope

Hope is not something you simply feel. It is something you choose, nurture, and practice every single day. Like a muscle, it strengthens through use and weakens through neglect. You cannot wait for hope to appear. You must build it into your life.

In moments when your faith feels thin or your courage wavers, you can return to a few simple practices that will help you guard and grow the flame of hope within you.

1. Remember What God Has Done

Write down the moments when God has been faithful in your past. Keep a "hope journal." Each answered prayer, each closed door that became protection, each trial that turned into triumph, record them. When the next storm comes, read those pages. Memory is the soil where hope takes root again.

2. Speak Life Over Your Future

Words create worlds. Proverbs 18:21 reminds us that life and death are in the power of the tongue. Begin your day by declaring God's promises rather than rehearsing your fears. Say out loud, "God is not finished with me yet." The atmosphere of your heart changes when your mouth agrees with hope.

3. Surround Yourself With Faith Builders

Hope grows in community. Spend time with people who speak faith, who remind you of your calling, and who lift your eyes higher when discouragement sets in. Isolation feeds despair. Connection revives courage.

4. Serve While You Wait

One of the fastest ways to reignite hope is to help someone else find theirs. Serving shifts your focus from what you lack to what you can give. When you pour into others, you discover that God replenishes what you thought you had lost.

5. Stay Anchored in God's Word

Scripture is the anchor of unshakable hope. When uncertainty surrounds you, God's Word becomes a steady foundation beneath your feet. Romans 15:13 declares, "May the God of hope fill you with all joy and peace as you trust in Him." Hope is not self-generated. It flows from trusting the One who cannot fail.

The Hope Declaration

As we close this journey, I invite you to speak this declaration of hope over your life:

"I will no longer be ruled by fear. I will forgive freely. I will value what God has placed within me. I will move forward with courage. And I will live with unshakable hope. My past no longer defines me. My future belongs to God."

Read those words slowly. Let them sink in. Hope is not wishful thinking; it is a holy confidence that God is still writing your story.

From Here to There

As you step into your next chapter, remember this: transformation is not a single moment but a continual choice. The R.E.A.C.H. journey, to Recognize, Embrace, Assess, Choose, and Hope, is not a one-time experience. It is a rhythm you can return to for the rest of your life.

Whenever fear whispers, recognize it.

When bitterness surfaces, embrace forgiveness.

When doubt says you have nothing, assess what is already in your house.

When hesitation returns, choose to begin again. And through it all, keep Hope alive.

Because the same God who started this work in you will be faithful to complete it. Philippians 1:6 promises, "He who began a good work in you will carry it on to completion until the day of Christ Jesus."

Hope is not the end of your story. It is the beginning of every new one that God is about to write through you.

Appendix: The 30-Day R.E.A.C.H. Journey

A Practical Guide to Living Your Transformation

Transformation does not happen in a single moment; it unfolds through consistent choices, one day at a time. The 30-Day R.E.A.C.H. Journey is designed to help you *live* what you have learned, to move from revelation to rhythm.

Each week focuses on one pillar of your journey: **Recognize. Embrace. Assess. Choose. Hope.**

Take your time. Some days will be light, others deeply reflective. Let the Holy Spirit set the pace.

Week 1: Recognize – Unmasking Fear

Theme: Awareness is the beginning of freedom.

- **Day 1:** Ask God to reveal the subtle ways fear hides in your life. Write them down honestly.
- **Day 2:** Reflect on a time when fear stopped you from stepping forward. What was the cost?
- **Day 3:** Read 2 Timothy 1:7. Write a short prayer asking God to replace fear with power, love, and a sound mind.

- **Day 4:** Journal: What triggers fear in you most, failure, rejection, loss, or uncertainty?
- **Day 5:** Invite accountability. Share one area of fear with a trusted friend or mentor.
- **Day 6:** Declare aloud: "Fear is not my future."
- **Day 7:** Sabbath reflection. Write three blessings that came this week as you faced your fears honestly.

Week 2: Embrace – The Liberation of Forgiveness

Theme: Forgiveness is freedom in motion.

- **Day 8:** Ask God to bring to mind anyone you need to forgive, including yourself.
- **Day 9:** Write their names in your journal. Beside each, write one thing you learned through that pain.
- **Day 10:** Pray the prayer of release: "Father, I place this person and this wound into Your hands."
- **Day 11:** Reflect: How has holding on to pain shaped your heart?
- **Day 12:** Write a letter of forgiveness (you do not have to send it).
- **Day 13:** Practice gratitude. Thank God for the growth that came through struggle.
- **Day 14:** Sabbath reflection. Note how forgiveness has lightened your spirit.

Week 3: Assess – Discovering Your Hidden Treasure

Theme: What you have is already enough when placed in God's hands.

- **Day 15:** List five skills or experiences that make you unique.
- **Day 16:** Ask, "What do I say 'nothing at all except' about in my life?"
- **Day 17:** Use the **Treasure Map Tool**, connect your gifts, passions, and experiences.
- **Day 18:** Ask a trusted friend what strengths they see in you that you might overlook.
- **Day 19:** Pray, "Lord, help me to see myself the way You see me."
- **Day 20:** Take one small action that uses one of your gifts.
- **Day 21:** Sabbath reflection. Write a testimony of how God has used something ordinary for something extraordinary.

Week 4: Choose – The Courage to Begin

Theme: Courage grows when you move.

- **Day 22:** Identify one thing you have been delaying. Write down why.
- **Day 23:** Commit to one small step forward today. Action breaks fear's grip.

- **Day 24:** Use the **Courage Compass Tool**, pray, clarify, count the cost, commit, and act.

- **Day 25:** Journal: What lies has "tomorrow" whispered to you? Replace each with God's truth.

- **Day 26:** Celebrate progress, even if it feels small. Movement matters.

- **Day 27:** Write a declaration: "Today, I choose courage over comfort."

- **Day 28:** Sabbath reflection. Record how obedience opened new doors this week.

Week 5: Hope – The Power to Move Forward

Theme: Hope is the anchor that keeps your heart steady and your faith alive.

- **Day 29:** Write down three promises from Scripture that fill you with hope.

- **Day 30:** Speak this declaration aloud:

"I will no longer be ruled by fear. I will forgive freely. I will value what God has placed within me. I will move forward with courage. And I will live with unshakable hope."

Close your 30-day journey with thanksgiving. Reflect on how far you have come and invite God to keep revealing what is next.

A Final Word

Your R.E.A.C.H. journey does not end here. It continues every time you recognize fear's disguise, embrace forgiveness, assess your gifts, choose to begin, and walk in hope.

Let this 30-day rhythm become a lifestyle. Let hope remain your compass, courage your step, and faith your steady song.

Because the world needs what God has placed within you, and it begins when you choose to R.E.A.C.H.

Epilogue

Released for Purpose

You have now walked the full R.E.A.C.H. journey.

You began by learning to recognize fear for what it is: a thief dressed in logic, comparison, and urgency. You unmasked its lies and saw that its voice was never God's voice.

You then chose to Embrace forgiveness, releasing chains that kept you bound to past wounds. You discovered that freedom was never about the apology you did or did not receive, but about trusting God enough to let go. From there, you learned to assess your hidden potential. Like the widow with her jar of oil, you saw that what you once dismissed as nothing could actually be the beginning of everything. You've discovered treasures buried in your skills, experiences, scars, and even your struggles.

You then made the decision to choose courage over comfort. You saw that tomorrow is not guaranteed and that delay has a cost. You began to take steps forward, not perfectly but faithfully, trusting that God multiplies movement more than hesitation.

And now, you arrive at the final piece: Hope. 4

Hope is not just the conclusion of your journey; it is the journey itself. Hope is the fuel that will carry you through the seasons ahead. Hope steadies you when fear resurfaces, when forgiveness feels costly, when your gifts feel small, and when the temptation to delay returns. Hope anchors your soul in storms and lifts your eyes toward promises that seem impossibly far away.

This is the power of being Released for Purpose.

R.E.A.C.H. is more than a framework. It is a way of living.

It is a rhythm of faith, courage, and resilience. It is the reminder that you have been called, equipped, and positioned for such a time as this.

So go forward with hope. Let your recognition sharpen your courage. Let your forgiveness free your heart. Let your assessment reveal your treasure. Let your choice to begin ignite your momentum. And let your hope keep you pressing forward when resistance comes.

The world is waiting for your contribution. Someone's healing is connected to your story. Someone's breakthrough is tied to your obedience. Someone's hope will awaken because you carried yours with confidence. You have been released for Purpose. Now go, and live it.

Next Steps and Connection

Freedom is not a finish line. It is the beginning of a new journey.

Your release from the chains that once held you is only the first step toward discovering the destiny God designed for you. The pages of this book may close, but your story of transformation continues.

You were never meant to walk alone. Purpose is refined in Community. Growth takes root through fellowship, mentorship, and accountability. It is within connection that freedom becomes strength and potential becomes legacy.

If this book has spoken to you, awakened something within you, or reminded you of who you truly are, I invite you to stay connected. There are ongoing resources, teachings, and encouragement designed to help you continue walking in the fullness of your God-given destiny.

Ways to Stay Connected

1. YouTube Channel

Join me on YouTube at **@R4Purpose** for weekly encouragement, video devotionals, and practical teaching on faith, identity, and purposeful living.

2. Website

Visit **www.R4Purpose.com** to explore articles, mentorship resources, upcoming events, and opportunities to grow in purpose and leadership.

3. Facebook

Connect with me at **facebook.com/kirk.campbell.568294** for daily inspiration, behind-the-scenes insights, and a growing community of believers who are walking in freedom and destiny together.

A Final Word

You were created for Purpose. You were redeemed for impact. And you are being released to live in divine rhythm with your destiny.

Do not let this moment fade into memory. Take one step today.

Reach out to someone who inspires you. Join a community of faith. Spend time in prayer and reflection. Continue to grow in grace and alignment.

Every act of obedience brings you closer to the life God intended.

Every decision to trust opens the door to transformation.

Stay connected. Stay aligned. Stay released.

Your best days are not behind you. They are waiting to be lived in step with God's purpose for your life.

www.ingramcontent.com/pod-product-compliance
Lightning Source LLC
Chambersburg PA
CBHW051328120626
46547CB00015B/2454